HORSES

ANIMAL FAMI

HORSES

Hans D. Dossenbach

Gareth Stevens Publishing
MILWAUKEE

A N I M A L   F A M I L I E S

For a free color catalog describing Gareth Stevens' list of high-quality books, call 1-800-341-3569 (USA) or 1-800-461-9120 (Canada).

The editor would like to thank Thomas E. Moore, Ph.D., Exhibit Museum Director, Curator of Insects, and Professor of Biology at the University of Michigan, Ann Arbor, Michigan, for his kind and professional help with the information in this book.

Library of Congress Cataloging-in-Publication Data

Dossenbach, Hans D., 1936-
    [Pferde. English]
    Horses / Hans D. Dossenbach.
      p. cm. — (Animal families)
    Translation of: Pferde
    Includes bibliographical references and index.
    Summary: Discusses the history, physical characteristics, and native environments of various wild and domestic members of the horse family.
    ISBN 0-8368-0841-X
    1. Equidae—Juvenile literature. [1. Equidae. 2. Horses.] I. Title.
  II. Series: Animal families (Milwaukee, Wis.)
QL737.U62D6713 1992
599.72'5—dc20   92-10658

North American edition first published in 1992 by
Gareth Stevens Publishing
1555 North RiverCenter Drive, Suite 201
Milwaukee, Wisconsin 53212, USA

Series editor: Patricia Lantier-Sampon
Editor: Barbara J. Behm
Translated from the German by Jamie Daniel
Editorial assistant: Diane Laska
Editorial consultant: Thomas E. Moore, Ph.D.

Printed in MEXICO

3 4 5 6 7 8 9 98 97 96

Table of Contents

What Is a Horse?

Opposite, illustration: The hoof (at left and center) is extremely tough. With little actual contact surface, the horse can easily bolt away from danger. A: coronary band, B: hoof wall, C: bulb, D: frog, E: hoof sole, F: support band. A standard horseshoe is also pictured: G: cleat hole, H: nail holes, I: toe cap.

Below: Horses in the wild prefer to live in herds, where they feel more secure.

The strong and fleet-footed horse has been the loyal companion and workmate of humans the world over for thousands of years. Whether for play or work, however, horses are fascinating animals to observe and care for. Maybe you are lucky enough to see horses often or even have the opportunity to ride them for fun. In any case, it is interesting that scientists know a great deal about the different members of the horse family — even more than they do about human beings.

Scientists, for example, understand why horses neigh, and they know how horses reproduce. They also know why humans have been able to master the horse in spite of the animal's greater strength.

Safety in Numbers

As a rule, horses in the wild live on wide, open grasslands. Because the area is so open, they have no way of protecting themselves from enemies such as wolves. The only thing the

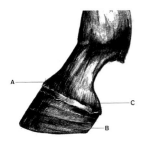

A ___
C ___
B ___
D ___
E ___
F ___
G ___
I ___
H ___

Below, top: Social grooming *is the term used when horses groom each others' coats.*

Below, center: A mare is ready to mate about every three weeks. Once a mare becomes pregnant by a stallion, it will carry a foal for eleven months.

Below, bottom: A foal comes into the world fully formed and ready to play.

horses can do is run away from the wolves. For this reason, a horse's entire body is built for speed and endurance. In addition, horses have excellent senses of hearing, smell, and sight. Their eyes arch forward and are set on the sides of their head. This makes it possible for them to look almost completely around without having to constantly turn their head. At the least sign of danger, a horse won't waste any time trying to decide what to do. It will react immediately by bolting away at full speed. This bolting is still instinctual, or natural, even after five thousand years of living with humans.

Anyone who has been around horses has probably seen how a slight noise or a scrap of paper blowing in the wind can cause a horse to bolt. For horses in the wild, this ability to react instantly can save the horse's life. It allows the horse to quickly escape danger.

The offspring of many animals are helpless during the first few weeks of their lives. Horses, however, are fast runners as soon as they are born. The mother carries her foal, or young, for eleven months. The horse is already quite well developed by the time it is born. It can stand up on wobbly legs and seek out its mother's milk just a few minutes after birth. It is usually strong enough to keep up with the adults by the next morning.

Even with all its strength, a young horse would have little chance of surviving if it lived on its own. Life in a herd can keep a horse

The domestic horse evolved from several different wild horses. The first ancestor of the true ponies was a small pony (left) that lived in the northern tundras and moors until the ice age began.

The most important ancestors of warm-bloods were the tarpans (center). The ancestors of cold-bloods were big cold-bloods (right).

safe. No danger goes unnoticed for long when there are so many sensitive eyes, ears, and noses on alert. Life in a herd also means that horses have to learn to get along with each

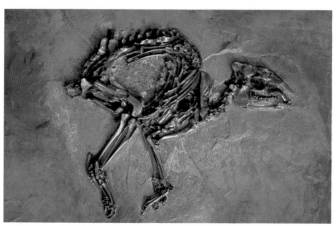

Above: The best specimen of an ancestral horse was found in an oil bed near Darmstadt in Germany. It is over fifty million years old. This rabbit-sized animal was called Propalaeotherium messelense.

other. They need a lead animal to guide the rest of the herd toward grassy areas with good living conditions.

Horses are also able to communicate with each other in a kind of common "language." Life in the herd is carried out through a series of different noises, postures, movements, and facial expressions. The loudest noise in

the language of horses is called the *neigh*. The neigh is a long, loud cry that keeps horses in touch with each other.

The "Marmot-like Animal"

One day in 1839 in England, naturalist William Richardson stumbled upon a small, primitive animal skull. He showed it to a zoologist named Richard Owen, who examined it carefully. Owen decided to call the unknown animal to whom the skull had once belonged *Hyracotherium* (or *Eohippus*), or "marmot-like animal." A marmot is a small, woodchuck type of animal. Looking back at his decision, no one could blame Owen for making this mistake, because the fist-sized skull with its small, ragged teeth did not look anything like what it really was — the head of a horse.

Fifty years later in Europe, Asia, and especially North America, a huge number of bones from extinct types of horses were discovered. To date, the earliest known remains of this small animal have been found in North American rocks dating back fifty-four million years. From these finds, it was eventually determined that the strange *Hyracotherium* (*Eohippus*) was the oldest known ancestor of today's horses. Scientists believe it lived about fifty million years ago.

A lighter-weight, longer-legged horse (left) with a big head that pushed forward was the ancestor of the Barbary horse, so important to the breeding of warm-bloods. The Arabians are thought to *have evolved from small, quick desert horses (center). The Przewalski's horse (right) apparently did not have a big role in the evolution of the domestic horse.*

From Life in the Swamps to the Plains

The *Hyracotherium* was no bigger than a rabbit. It did not have hooves initially, but instead had toes that could spread apart. The *Hyracotherium* probably lived in swamps, where its toes would protect it from sinking into the mud. In time, the giant mud flats dried up in Europe, northern Asia, and North America. As a result, many animals, including several early forms of horses, died out. Some types of animals were able to adapt, or change, in order to survive the new conditions. The horses that did survive changed over the course of millions of years into large, fast animals that lived in dry, open areas.

About ten thousand years ago, toward the end of the last ice age, the first wild horses had spread over almost all of the Americas, Asia, Europe, and northern Africa. Different groups of horses, called *subspecies*, appeared. The subspecies were different from each other in their build, size, and temperament. These differences developed because of the different living conditions of each region. Small, short-legged ponies and huge, powerful horses were found in the north. The horse that resembles today's Przewalski's horse lived on the plains of central Asia. In the desert areas of the Near East, the delicate and fast desert

Below: These Dülmener wild horses (upper) live at a wild stable in Germany. They are one of the original breeds of horses. The Exmoor pony (lower) can be seen in southwestern England. It is a breed of pony that has been kept almost completely pure.

Below: This representation of a horse's head is over ten thousand years old. It was found on the wall of a cave in northern Spain. The horse was not used for hunting at the time but was itself hunted by humans.

Left, upper: A Greek coin shows Pegasus, a legendary winged horse. Left, lower: Macedonian King Philipp in his horse-drawn chariot 2,300 years ago. Below: This "flying horse" was made of bronze two thousand years ago in China.

breeds were found. All of these wild horses were tamed sooner or later by humans and often moved from one place to another. This accounts for the variety of features on the many different breeds of horses.

How People and Horses Got Together

In 1879, a great number of horse paintings were discovered on the walls of the Altamira Cave in northern Spain. At that time, no one realized that these works of art had been painted during the ice age. Only in 1902, when more such paintings were found in France, did scientists determine that the paintings dated back from ten thousand to thirty thousand years ago. The paintings were not meant to simply decorate the caves of these early people. Instead, they had some sort of religious purpose; they were done to please the gods and bring luck to the hunt.

Scientists still are not sure when the horse became a domestic, or tame, animal. Goats, sheep, cattle, and even llamas were all domesticated before the horse.

People began keeping horses for the first time about five thousand years ago. Some experts believe the earliest keepers of horses were nomads, or wanderers, who crossed the great plains north of the Caucasus mountain range on the border of Europe and Asia. This area was home to the plains tarpan, a breed of wild horse that became extinct sometime during the early twentieth century. The plains tarpan was the very first domestic horse.

Roles of Horses in War and Peace

The people who first kept horses north of the Caucasus Mountains were warlike. About 3,500 years ago, they left their native plains to wage war. They had a weapon that no one was able to match — battle wagons that were pulled by teams of horses. These people kept written records on tablets of their attacks on neighbors. The oldest known records of domestic horses are found on these tablets. Some historians believe that the horses of these times were first used to pull wagons. They believe that only later were the horses

A German knight wearing light armor around 1498. In battle, both men and horses had to wear heavy metal armor for protection.

Napoleon on his Arabian stallion, Vizir. The horse is said to have carried Napoleon from France to Moscow and back again.

This painting by Swiss painter Karl Bodmer shows a member of the Blackfoot Indian tribe in North America on a spirited Spanish horse.

ridden. But it is also possible that early cattle herders rode horses, making this the first domestic use of horses by people.

Domestic horses were soon found in the area bordering the eastern Mediterranean Sea. As early as three thousand years ago, Egyptians and Trojans used horses to pull their battle wagons, or chariots. One hundred years later, Indians and Greeks were doing the same. The Egyptians had soldiers on horseback 3,300 years ago. During the same period, people in western Europe were also beginning to keep horses — but just as a source of food. They did not use wagons and did not realize yet that horses could be ridden.

For almost four thousand years, the horse has had a greater effect on human history than any other animal. The fierce battles led by Genghis Kahn, Alexander the Great, Julius Caesar, Hernando Cortés, Napoleon Bonaparte, and other prominent military men would have been impossible without horses.

The peaceful use of horses by humans has also been significant. Hunters and livestock herders rode horses because of the animals' speed and endurance. Farmers valued horses as powerful, untiring work animals. Horses made it possible for people and goods to be transported over great distances. Horses also made it possible for postal systems to develop. Before electricity and the gas engine were invented, horses pulled streetcars through towns and ships through channels. It is no wonder that the output of a motor is measured in "horsepower."

Who Has the Fastest Horse?

Sports involving horses are as old as riding itself. Centuries ago, sheepherders challenged each other to races to find out who had the fastest horse. In ancient Greece, horse races were among the most popular sports, and chariot races were the most popular attraction at the Olympic Games from the year 680 B.C. on. Forty years later, there was also an Olympic category for races with riders. The best riders and horses were honored just like today's sports heroes.

Two men race their swift Arabian horses across the desert.

In ancient times, the fastest and strongest horses were chosen for breeding. This, of course, resulted in the births of horses that were even faster and stronger than their parents. Horse breeding is not done to simply produce more horses but also to produce breeds of the highest possible quality.

Who Is the Best Rider?

Over time, many different riding games and skills developed all over the world. Speed was important, but so was skilled riding. The herders who raced against each other did not race just to see who could be the fastest from one point to another. They also raced to see who could use the most skill and grace in doing so.

Soldiers in various countries also competed in events that were held to practice the skills used in battle. Roman soldiers, for example, speared a wooden stake with their swords while riding. Knights during the Middle Ages tried to knock each other from their saddles with lances. Austrian soldiers speared dummy heads while riding at a gallop. The most advanced riding games were developed by the soldiers in India. These exercises were known as *gymkhana* and were eventually brought to Europe by the British. They require a great degree of skill, including the ability to react quickly and to establish excellent coordination between rider and horse.

Recreational Riding

Most horses can be easily trained to obey signals given by people. Horses have good

Below, upper: Horse jumping is a favorite sport involving horses in central Europe.

Below, lower: Rodeos are festivals that developed out of the everyday work activities of North American cowboys.

memories, and they can learn various commands. They work hard to please their owners or trainers.

Recreational riding, or riding for pleasure, is one of the most popular tasks horses have been trained to perform over the centuries. *Recreational riding* is the term used when people take part in horseback riding as well as in competitive and distance riding, exercises of skill, and riding games.

For example, polo is a ball game that people play on horseback. Polo horses or polo ponies are not of any special breed or size. It takes several years to train a horse to play the game of polo. The horse is trained to stop quickly, and to turn, twist, and resume stride without losing speed. The game probably began about two thousand years ago in Persia, present-day Iran. It was introduced into England in 1869 and into the United States in 1876.

Parts of the horse's body are illustrated on page 15.

1: neck; 2: shoulder; 3: mane; 4: withers; 5: back; 6: rump or crupper; 7: base of tail; 8: thigh; 9: tail; 10: knee; 11: hock; 12: fetlocks; 13: pastern; 14: hoof; 15: hoof coronet; 16: front leg joint; 17: chest; 18: rear section of lower jaw; 19: upper and lower lip; 20: nostrils; 21: eye; 22: forehead; 23: ear.

Przewalski's Horse

Fjord Horse

Domestic Horse (Warm-blood)

Domestic Ass (Donkey)

Plains, or Burchell's, Zebra

A Guide to Horses

African Wild Ass

Grevy's Zebra

Asiatic Wild Ass

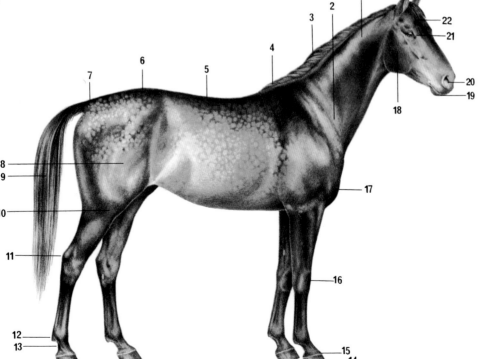

Przewalski's Horses

Height: 48-52 inches (122-132 cm)
Height in hands: 12-13
Place of origin: Western Mongolia

The Przewalski's horse is the only breed of wild horse that has survived into the present. Wild horses such as the forest tarpan that lived all across Europe and the plains tarpan that lived in southern Russia became extinct in the early twentieth century. Today's Exmoor pony (pictured on page 9) is descended from these animals.

Przewalski's horses lived on the vast plains of central Asia and in the deserts west of the Ural Mountains at the border of Europe and Asia. These horses were last seen in the wild over twenty years ago in the remote areas of the Gobi Desert in Asia. Fortunately, there are still Przewalski's horses in zoos around the world, and pairs of these horses are brought together for breeding in order to save them from extinction. In this way, the total number of these rare horses has increased to about seven hundred. Przewalski's horses range in color from sandy to reddish brown. Their manes stand straight up and have no forelock, or long hair, in the front of the head.

Wild Domestic Horses

The Mustang:
Height: 56 inches (142 cm)
Height in hands: 12-13
Weight: 600-800 pounds (270-365 kg)
Place of origin: United States

Certain horses are considered wild. These include the mustang, the Dulmener wild horse, the "wild horses of Camargue," and the "wild ponies of Assateague." In truth, none of these are true wild horses. Rather, they are domestic horses that have returned to life in the wild.

Mustangs — the "Big Dogs" of the American Indians

North America is one part of the earth where horses originally evolved, or developed. But

Above, left: Przewalski's horse — the last real wild horse — can now only be seen in captivity. People are trying to save it through breeding programs.
Above, right: The Dülmeners of northern Germany resemble both the extinct wild tarpan and the Exmoor pony.
Opposite: North America's wild horses, the mustangs, are actually domestic horses that have gone wild. They descend from Spanish horses that came to the Americas with Spanish explorers.

they died out in North America about eight thousand years ago. No one knows why this happened. Horses were first seen again in the Americas when the conquerors from Spain arrived. And when Christopher Columbus made his second voyage to the New World, he brought along thirty horses. Almost every other Spanish ship that followed him to the Americas during the sixteenth century brought more horses.

American Indians of that time were shocked to see Spanish soldiers riding horses. The Indians thought the horses and riders were magical beings, half human and half animal. When the Indians realized the beings were two separate creatures, they naturally wanted horses of their own. Horses allowed the Indians to be better hunters and warriors.

The Indians quickly became experts at handling horses, but they did not realize at first that horses needed to be fenced in. Many of their horses ran off to live in the wild all across the American West, from Mexico in the south to Canada in the north. By 1900, there were an estimated two million of these horses, called *mustangs*, in the wild. But these horses were constantly pushed back by settlers who had also killed off the millions of buffalo that had once roamed the prairies. Hundreds of thousands of mustangs were captured and tamed, then ridden to their deaths on the battlefields of the Civil War. Hundreds of thousands more were killed and made into cat food, dog food, chicken feed, and even fertilizer. In addition, hundreds of thousands more mustangs were killed by livestock herders who wanted to make sure that only their livestock grazed on the grass. Because of all this destruction, there were only eight thousand mustangs left by 1970.

Today, about twenty thousand mustangs roam the American West. It is against the law to kill these horses.

The Shipwreck Survivors of Assateague
During the sixteenth century, a Spanish ship was attacked off the eastern coast of North America. It ran aground on the rocks and

Above: The famous white horses of the Camargue in southern France.
Left, upper: Costenas in the Peruvian Andes live at 9,843 feet (3,000 m) above sea level.
Left, lower: A wild pony on the island of Assateague off the coast of the eastern United States.

Assateague is still home only to horses, mosquitoes, and great numbers of birds. But each year, people from the neighboring island of Chincoteague capture several young ponies and tame them for work and trade.

Wild Horses the World Over
Horses are adaptable animals, able to survive in extreme climates and conditions. Herds of domestic horses that have gone wild can be found in many parts of the world, from the plains of central Asia to the Australian bush country. They must find their own food and rarely come into contact with people. Herds also roam the marshes and mountains of France and Spain, the moors of England, Scotland, and Ireland, and areas of Iceland, Scandinavia, and Germany.

sank. None of the people on board survived, but several horses managed to swim to an island off the coast called Assateague. The animals adapted to the tough swamp grass, the swarms of mosquitos during hot summers, and the ice storms during cold winters. Life on the island was not easy, and only the strongest horses — mainly the smaller ones — survived and reproduced. This explains why the wild horses on Assateague grew only to the size of ponies.

Ponies

Height: 32-58 inches (81-148 cm)
Height in hands: 8-14
Weight: 450-850 pounds (204-386 kg)

Ponies can make good pets for children. They are gentle animals that learn quickly. They can be ridden, and they are able to pull small carts. Ponies feed on grass and hay and usually live longer than other types of horses.

When most people hear the word pony, they think of a sturdy, short-legged little horse with lots of hair on its mane and tail. This is a good description of a Shetland pony. But the Connemara pony from Ireland and the Bosnian mountain pony look quite different from the Shetland pony.

In sports that involve horses, any horse shorter than 58 inches (148 cm) at the withers is considered a pony. But this rule only applies to sports. Many desert Arabians measure less than 58 inches (148 cm) at the withers, and yet they are the most perfect of thoroughbred horses.

One of the smallest ponies is the Shetland pony, which stands from 32 to 46 inches (81

The Shetland pony is the most popular pony among children.

to 117 cm) high. It developed two thousand years ago on the Shetland Islands, north of Scotland. The ponies had to be very hardy to survive the damp and cold climate. Shetland ponies were first used as pack animals, but some were later taken to England to work in the coal mines.

The powerful Icelandic pony is a favorite with adults as well as children.

Over time, the Shetland pony has become very popular throughout the United States. It is sure-footed and generally has a gentle temperament.

What Is a Pony?

From a scientist's point of view, the pony is a very specific type of domestic horse. Its features were once found in certain northern European wild horses. Today, these same features are found in the breeds born of the first ponies known as northern ponies or northern horses.

The first ponies were well adapted to life in the cold, damp climate of northern Europe. They had wide and very powerful molars with long roots. These teeth made it possible for the horses to bite off and chew even the toughest weeds. The type of food they could find had little nutritional value. Therefore, the ponies had to eat large quantities of it in order to get the nutrients their bodies needed.

The ponies also had to have large digestive systems, which is why they had big, barrel-shaped upper bodies. Their heads were short with a wide forehead and big eyes. Their ears were small and covered with thick hair to protect them from the cold. Their short legs were not built for speed but rather for strength to help them cross the rough countryside. Their manes and tails were covered with thick, coarse hair. Their coats were coarse and oily and had a thick woolly undercoat during the winter. The horses were well protected from the cold and damp because of these features.

Today, there are a number of pony breeds that still have all of these features. These include the Shetland, Icelandic, and Exmoor ponies. Many pony breeds, however, have been interbred, or crossbred, with big horses, especially with English and Arabian Thoroughbreds. The British have been able to breed new types of ponies that do not even look like ponies of the past. There are many Welsh ponies, for example, that look like mini-Arabian horses. They are beautiful small horses that sometimes have moody and unpleasant temperaments.

About twenty years ago, there were hardly any other ponies in central Europe except the Shetlands, and these ponies were seen mostly in zoos and circuses. Then the larger ponies that were well-suited for adult riders began to be seen more often. The Icelandic ponies were the first to be discovered by the Europeans for recreational riding purposes. These sturdy little horses were followed by various breeds of all shapes and sizes. Especially popular were breeds from Great Britain, the classic home of ponies, and breeds from Scandinavia.

There are over fifty types of ponies. They include the following:

Shetland Pony

Shetland ponies are the smallest breed of horse, with an average height of 40 inches (102 cm). The ponies have been untiring workhorses for the local inhabitants of the Shetland Islands off the coast of Scotland for centuries. They have a friendly temperament, although they can be quite stubborn.

Icelandic Pony

Icelandic ponies are larger than the Shetlands, standing about 51 inches (130 cm) at the withers. They are strong enough to carry an adult on their backs, and they have become one of the favorite recreational ponies in Europe. Special varieties of Icelandic ponies are shown in competition. Icelandic ponies have been bred on Iceland for over one thousand years.

English Moor Pony

Dartmoor ponies live on the moors of Devon, England. They grow approximately 47 inches (120 cm) tall and closely resemble the Shetland pony. The Dartmoor pony is a favorite of children because of its calm temperament.

Exmoor ponies are also found in Great Britain. These ponies live mainly in a semi-wild state in forests, moors, and heaths.

Welsh Pony

Welsh ponies are descended from small Celtic ponies, with an average height of 48 inches (122 cm). Some of these ponies are very

delicate, while others are built quite powerfully.

Connemara Pony

The Irish Connemara ponies also descend from Celtic animals. They are usually between 51 to 57 inches (130 to 145 cm) tall and have

Opposite: Connemara ponies in Ireland.
Right, top: Macedonian mountain pony.
Right, center: A Welsh pony that clearly has Arabian forebears.
Right, bottom: The "pony of the Americas" (POA), a new, speckled pony breed from the United States.

sturdy features that make them extremely well adapted for use in sports.

Fjord Pony

The Fjord pony is descended from Viking horses. It is strong, even-tempered, and reliable. Norwegians bred Viking horses with cold-blooded horses to produce a muscular workhorse standing 51 to 57 inches (130 to 145 cm) tall. Because good riding ponies are in great demand, a smaller variety of the Fjord horse has been bred over the last twenty years for riding.

Gotlander Pony

The Gotlander pony is almost unknown outside its native Sweden. It measures between 44 and 52 inches (112 and 132 cm) in height, has a good temperament, and makes an excellent riding horse for both adults and children. It appears to have descended directly from horses that once lived on Gotland Island in the Baltic Sea.

Bosnian Mountain Pony

Bosnian mountain ponies are sure-footed and sturdy. At 53 inches (135 cm) tall, these little horses are valuable to farmers and the military. Several thousand Bosnian mountain ponies have been brought into Europe recently for use as recreational horses.

Above: The Fjord pony traditionally has its mane clipped. No one knows how this began or whether it really is good for the horse.
Left: The even-tempered Dartmoor pony shows the influence of the Shetland pony.

Opposite, left: The Shire horse is the largest of all the cold-blooded horses. Stallions can be over 6.5 feet (2 m) in height and weigh over 2,860 pounds (1,300 kg).
Opposite, right: The Suffolk Punch is an equally powerful British horse.

Cold-blooded Horses

Height: 62-65 inches (157-165 cm)
Height in hands: 15.2-16.1
Weight: 1,350-2,205 pounds (612-1,000 kg)

Thirty years ago, a Danish economist predicted that horses would be found only in museums and zoos after 1980. Fortunately, he was wrong — even if it did seem at the time as if the domestic horse was fast on its way to disappearing.

For example, in 1940, there were sixty thousand Swedish-Ardenner mares being bred in Sweden. By 1976, there were only 1,700 left. The population had decreased by 97 percent. This situation was much the same all over western Europe, where the horsepower of engines was replacing the power of working horses. Big, powerful cold-blooded horses began to disappear from country roads and farms. But they are far from extinct.

What Is a Cold-blooded Horse?

Ancestors of today's cold-blooded horses could be found in the barren lands of the north. They were huge, wild horses with heavy heads, powerful upper bodies with plenty of room for digesting food, and muscular legs with big hooves that would not sink into the marshy ground. These horses were about 55 to 70 inches (140 to 178 cm) at the withers, the biggest by far of the wild horses. Many experts assume that all present-day cold-blooded horses descended from them.

The body temperature of a cold-blooded horse is the same as that of a warm-blooded horse. Their names, therefore, are misleading. The name *cold-blooded* is meant to describe the peaceful, cool temperaments of horses, not their blood temperature. Typical features of the cold-bloods include their medium to very heavy builds and their strong legs with large hooves that are often concealed by hair. In addition, these horses have very powerful necks and very large, heavy heads. They range in height from a small 60 inches (150 cm) to over 72 inches (182 cm).

Cold-blooded horses are mainly workhorses. Many of them weigh more than 1,760 pounds (800 kg), and some as much as 2,200 pounds (1,000 kg). Lighter, more graceful types are also bred mainly in mountainous regions, where they are used for pulling. Examples of these mountain horses include the Freibergers from Switzerland and the blond Tirolean Haflingers from Austria.

They Continue to Work

Northern France was once the center of cold-blooded horse breeding. Here and there in

northern France, you might see a powerful horse called the Trait du Nord, or a Percheron, Breton, or Ardenne. These were horses that had an influence on horse breeding all over the world. But now, many young people in central Europe have never even seen a cold-blooded horse. These horses can only be seen at times in remote mountain villages.

Approximately 15,000 of the 35,000 horses in Austria are Norikers — representatives of one of the oldest breeds of cold-bloods. The smaller Haflingers are also being bred there, and their numbers are increasing. This is not only because they make such good workhorses, but also because they are widely used for recreational riding.

In highly modernized Switzerland, nearly 65 percent of all horses are cold-bloods. Most of these horses are still being used as work animals by the people who live there. Anyone who has seen the horses pulling logs from the mountain forests down to the valleys below understands they are superior to the modern tractor for such work and are, therefore, quite valuable. About 150 breed mares have seen to it that the reliable Freiberger horses will not become endangered animals.

There are still many workhorses in use in the forests and on the farms of northern Scandinavia. Of the 45,000 horses in Norway, approximately 30,000 are working Dole horses. Many Fjord horses are also used as workhorses there.

In the countries of eastern Europe, workhorses pulling wagons on the street are still common. However, only a few cold-bloods can be seen in countries such as Hungary, as almost all of the pull-teams are made up of warm-blooded horses. Cold-blooded horses have no tradition in Hungary.

The situation is similar in Poland, which has around three million horses. Poland has the largest population of horses in Europe. This country is best known for its Arabian horses, as well as for Polish Anglo-Arabians and the Polish Trakehners.

These proud horses are mostly sold in foreign markets, since Poland itself still needs workhorses more than any other type. As in Hungary, Polish workhorses are usually not cold-bloods, but usually Koniks. *Konik* is the Polish word for "little horse." This is an appropriate name for these untiring helpers of Poland's farmers. They are the size of ponies and are very tough, hard-working horses. They still have a lot of tarpan blood in their veins and often look just like these ancestral wild horses.

A Horse Called Tractor

In Russia, more cold-blooded horses can be found than anywhere else in the world. Of the approximately eight million horses in this country, no less than six-and-a-half million are cold-bloods. While workhorses are becoming increasingly rare elsewhere in the world, new breeds such as the so-called "Byelorussian," or "White Russian," are being bred in Russia. Already existing Russian cold-bloods were crossbred with workhorses from France, Belgium, Norway, Sweden, and England combined with a touch of Arabian blood to keep the end result from being too heavy and awkward. The result was a horse about 59 inches (150 cm) high that had a good temperament and could work hard. It was nicknamed *Tractor* by the Russian people.

Opposite: Scottish Clydesdales are among the most impressive cold-bloods. Right, upper: The Haflinger is a popular recreational horse. Right, lower: The Freiberger from Jura in Switzerland is highly valued as a workhorse.

Warm-blooded Horses

Height: 65-71 inches (165-180 cm)
Height in hands: 16-17
Weight: 1,000-1,400 pounds (453-635 kg)

What Is a Warm-blood?

Warm-blooded horses are much more spirited and quick to react than the cold-bloods. Instead of being bred for working purposes, the warm-bloods are the modern-day sports horses. These horses are developed specifically for leisure activities.

The equestrian, or horseback riding, competitions at Olympic Games today include training exercises, jumping, and military drills.   These three events, and especially jumping, are the favorites among the many sports involving horses. Breeders of sport horses try to produce animals especially talented at jumping and performing training exercises. They hope to produce a horse that is big, powerful, and "noble." A horse is considered noble if it has the temperament, speed, endurance, and elegance of the English and Arabian Thoroughbreds. These breeding goals have led to a large horse between 65 and 71 inches (165 and 180 cm) high.

The English and Arabian Thoroughbreds are warm-bloods, although the term *hot-blooded* is sometimes used to describe Arabians, too. The mixed breeds, or horses that are only half Thoroughbred, can also be classified as warm-bloods. Over two hundred different breeds of horses — two-thirds of all the breeds that exist in the world — are warm-bloods.

Above: Hungarian warm-bloods are modern horses bred for sport riding.
Opposite, left bottom: Knabstrupers are horses with Spanish ancestry.
Opposite, right top: The Lippizaners are first-class show horses.

Various types of wild horses contributed to the gradual evolution of the warm-bloods, especially the forest and plains tarpans.

Barbary and European Show Horses

One type of wild horse about which little is known lived in the mountainous regions of northwest Africa. It was a big, long-legged, quick horse. It had a long head that bulged on the top so that its eyes were set at a great distance from its nostrils. This horse preferred to either avoid people or attack them, a feature that is still common in today's "ram's headed" horses.

The Berbers, a tribe of nomads that lived in the desert mountains of North Africa, tamed these wild horses and eventually bred them into a spirited and fierce horse — the Barbary horse.

During the seventh century, the Arabs conquered great sections of territory east and south of the Mediterranean Sea on their lightning-fast horses. Among the peoples they conquered were the Berbers. This was actually a good thing for the breeding of Barbary horses. The strongest features of the spirited Barbary horses were brought out, or strengthened, by breeding them with

the fleet Arabian horses. They even became easier to handle.

When Islamic riders stormed over the Straits of Gibraltar to Spain and the Iberian Peninsula in the eighth century, they brought their horses with them. These horses were so good that they left their mark on horse breeding all over Europe. These were the Barbary horses that had been crossbred with Arabian horses. The Andalusian horses of southern Spain are among their descendants. These extremely elegant horses have proud, expressive movements and fiery tempers. The Neapolitan horse of southern Italy descended from the Andalusians.

Mustangs and almost all breeds of ponies that arrived in the Americas during the sixteenth century have developed from these same Spanish horses. The American horses have turned out to be wonderful warm-bloods with good tempers, excellent riding qualities, and extraordinary endurance.

have anything to do with the earlier Frederiksborgs that were first bred in the sixteenth century. There are, however, still horses on the north of Seeland Island in Denmark that look like the original parade horses. These are the Knabstrups. These horses have white coats with numerous small

In 1562, the Danish king Frederick II founded his royal stables at Frederiksborg, north of Copenhagen, with stallions carefully chosen from the best horses of Spain and Italy. The Frederiksborg horses that were bred at the royal stable and separated according to color became known throughout Europe as striking parade horses.

Today, there are still horses in Denmark called Frederiksborgs. These are completely modern, interbred sport horses that no longer

black or brown splotches, which are their so-called "dapple" marks. It is said that a Spanish officer sold a dappled mare to a Danish butcher in 1812. The butcher decided not to slaughter the animal with the unusual markings and instead sold it to a certain

Above: American standard trotters are among the most successful racehorses.

Opposite: Andalusians were once parade horses. Today they are used mainly for sports.

Knabstrup estate. There it went on to become the mother of a new breed of horses that has survived into the present.

The Kladruber breed was also begun with Andalusian and Neapolitan horses. Kladrubers are large coach horses. The ram's headed, black-and-white Kladrubers are still

show movements. The "dancing Lippizaners" of the famous Knie Circus are known and admired all over Europe.

At the Spanish Riding School in Vienna, only pure white horses are presented. But not all Lippizaners are white. In certain places where these horses wear harnesses

bred today in lesser numbers.

Of all of the parade horse breeds, the Lippizaners are by far the best known. The white stallions of the Spanish Riding School in Vienna, Austria, are world famous. The breed was founded in 1580 at Lippiza, a town near the city of Trieste, which was once part of the Austrian empire but now belongs to Italy. Lippizaners are bred mainly as show horses and are noted for their strength, elegance, and ability to perform complex

and often have to do strenuous agricultural work, coat color is not so important. Here the Lippizaners can be brown, reddish brown, and black. The main color of these workhorses is gray.

Modern Sport Horses

Germany has been especially successful in breeding modern warm-blooded horses for sports. In particular, the Hanoverians and their close relatives, the Holsteiners, are gifted show jumpers — and this is what is most in demand by riders and owners alike. But the best jumpers by far are the Wurttembergers. These French Anglo-Norman horses, which were greatly influenced by English thoroughbreds, have also been successful in several international competitions. The Wurttembergers are now bred in many other countries, including Switzerland. The Swedish warm-blooded horses are also extremely talented in performing training exercises for shows.

The Irish have an extremely powerful workhorse in their Irish Draught. But in order to produce a horse for hunting, they breed their Draught mares with thoroughbred English stallions. The result is the heavy-set Irish Hunter, especially well-suited to competitive sports. A *hunter* is basically a type of horse that can carry riders of different weights and sizes easily and comfortably over a certain terrain during hunting season. And in order to produce horses that are not only solid but also suitable for jumping, these Irish Hunters are bred in turn with English thoroughbreds. This results in a lighter, or at least intermediate weight, horse.

Above: The speckled Appaloosas were bred by North American Indians.

Left: This checkered horse from the North American West is called a pinto.

A smaller Irish Hunter is also produced when Ireland's Connemara pony mares are bred with thoroughbred stallions. The amazing Irish Hunter is one of the most successful jumping horses in the world.

English sports horses are, for the most part, the direct products of English thoroughbred stallions and warm-blooded mares. This combination has thus far produced the most desirable equine qualities for sports.

Arabians

Height: 57-61 inches (144-155 cm)
Height in hands: 14.1-15.1
Weight: 850-1,000 pounds (385-454 kg)
Place of origin: Arabian Peninsula

The Bedouin people in the Arabian highlands were desert-dwelling nomads who needed tough, fast horses that could endure harsh conditions. In order to get these qualities in their horses, they chose only the best horses for breeding. The horses that finally produced these qualities also turned out to be great beauties.

An Arabian stallion reigns over its natural environment.

Many fascinating legends try to explain the history of Arabian horses. One such story states that all Arabian thoroughbreds descend from one of the seven favorite mares of the Islamic prophet Mohammed. Known for its endurance, intelligence, and character, the breed had developed in Arabia by the seventh century. These magnificent horses, often less than 59 inches (150 cm) high, are the most important in the history of horse breeding.

Almost all warm-blood breeds as well as many breeds of pony and cold-bloods have been improved by crossbreeding with Arabians. The horses are faster, more mobile and spirited, better able to endure harsh conditions, and also more beautiful.

The designation "thoroughbred Arabian" or "Arabian thoroughbred" can only be used for horses whose ancestors are exclusively desert Arabians.

31

Thoroughbreds

Height: 63-70 inches (160-175 cm)
Height in hands: 15-17
Place of origin: Britain

From the fifteenth century on, many Arabians and other Oriental horses were brought to England. There they were bred with horses and ponies from England to produce faster racehorses for British riding sports. Around 1700, English Thoroughbred breeding was begun. The basis for this breed consisted of several dozen extremely fast mares and only three stallions: Godolphin Barb, a Barbary horse from Tunisia; Byerly Turk, an Oriental horse from Turkey; and Darley Arabian, probably a Thoroughbred Arabian. All of the English Thoroughbreds in the world — and there are approximately 750,000 of them — descend from these three stallions and their mares. Only horses whose ancestry can be traced in the official record book for the breed, called the General Stud Book, can be referred to as English Thoroughbreds. A descendant of Darley Arabian was brought to Virginia in the United States in the early part of the eighteenth century. This became the foundation of Thoroughbred breeding in the United States.

The Thoroughbred is between 63 and 70 inches (160 and 175 cm) high. It is the most important horse for racing and one of the best military and jumping horses in the world. The Thoroughbred has also been used for centuries to improve other breeds. The modern sport horse that is bred all over the world owes its features and beauty to the Thoroughbred.

The Thoroughbred — the fastest runner and most important horse in breeding racehorses.

Anglo-Arabian Horses

Height: 65-67 inches (165-170 cm)
Height in hands: 16.1-16.3

Three types of Anglo-Arabians have developed separately from each other. The Pompadour stables in Southern France were crossbreeding Arabians and Barbary horses in 1750. Around 1872, the royal stables in France also began to breed Anglo-Arabians. These horses continue to be bred in many countries and are among the most outstanding

Polish Anglo-Arabians, also known as Malopolskas.

One of the horses resulting from the interbreeding of English and Arabian thoroughbreds is the Anglo-Arabian. It stands 65 to 67 inches (165 to 170 cm) tall. The mingling of the two breeds has produced a horse that has a less moody, more friendly temperament than the English thoroughbred, and a greater talent for jumping than the Arabian. The Anglo-Arabian is an excellent sporting horse.

horses for use in sports.

The Hungarian Anglo-Arabian, known as the Gidran, developed around 1820. It looks more like the Arabian side of its lineage than the English side. Finally, there is the Polish Anglo-Arabian, known as the Malopolska. It was produced with Shagya Arabians and Gidrans from Hungary as well as Anglo-Arabians from France. The Malopolska is the most important Polish sporting horse.

Zebras

Height: 49-63 inches (124-160 cm)
Height in hands: 12-15
Weight: 660-990 pounds (300-450 kg)

North America and eventually to Central and South America as well. These people evolved into the various Indian tribes. Many animals also wandered from Asia to the Americas. These included a wild bison that evolved into the buffalo on the American prairies, and red deer that later evolved into the powerful Wapiti, or elk.

The northern subspecies of plains zebra called the Grant's zebra has a clearly marked black-and-white striped coat.

Like the first wild horses — and their descendants, domestic horses — zebras and asses descend from small, horselike animals that evolved in North America millions of years ago. Zebras and asses are now found in Europe, Africa, and Asia because they traveled there from North America over a land bridge that no longer exists. Today, this area is called the Bering Strait, a narrow strait of water between the northeastern tip of Asia and the northwestern tip of North America. Because of the land bridge that was once there, people were able to travel from Asia to

Many animals also traveled in the opposite direction. These included the ancestors of horses that spread eventually from Asia to Europe and Africa.

Bones of horses that lived ten thousand years ago show that American Indians ate horses for food. These American horses died out about eight thousand years ago and no one knows exactly why. The Indians are certainly not to blame for this, because they would never hunt their prey animals to extinction. This would have left them without a source of food. The white race is the only race that has killed off entire species of animals. Many experts believe that a natural disaster wiped out the first horses in North America, not the American Indians.

While the horses in North America were disappearing, those in Asia, Europe, and Africa began to thrive. They only ran into trouble a few thousand years later when people began to hunt them down in such numbers that many types are now threatened with extinction or are already extinct. This situation became worse with the invention of the long-distance rifle. Only one zebra, the plains zebra, still survives in great numbers in eastern and southeastern Africa.

The Plains, or Burchell's, Zebra

Today, it is possible to see great numbers of plains zebras in eastern Africa. Also referred to as Burchell's zebras, these animals often graze with herds of gnus, antelopes, gazelles, and giraffes. In the Serengeti, a huge national park in Tanzania in East Africa, there are about 180,000 zebras. Their territory extends over all of eastern and southern Africa.

There are five subspecies of the plains zebra. The groups have different coloring and markings. A sixth subgroup, the quagga, has died out. It was brown, with black-and-white stripes on its head, neck, and upper back. It lived in South Africa, a country where white settlers hunted down whatever native animals crossed their paths. The last quagga in the wild was shot dead in 1878. And in 1883, the last quagga on earth died in the Amsterdam Zoo in the Netherlands.

The most common subspecies of plains zebra is the Grant's zebra, which lives in eastern Africa. It has a black-and-white striped pattern over its entire body. It reaches a height of 51 inches (130 cm) at the withers and can weigh up to 660 pounds (300 kg).

Above, right: A Chapman's zebra, a subspecies of the plains zebra, patiently nurses her young.

The Mountain Zebra

Only 49 inches (125 cm) tall but weighing up to 660 pounds (300 kg), the mountain zebra is the smallest zebra. This group has two subspecies. The Cape Mountain Zebra lives in the South African Capeland and was barely saved from extinction. The last twenty-seven of the animals left during the 1950s were

gathered together in a nature preserve where they were able to greatly increase their numbers. There are now believed to be about 220 of the animals. The Hartmann's zebra lives in southwestern Africa and is also a fairly rare animal. Only a few thousand of these still survive.

Unlike the plains zebras that live in big herds and gather together in groups numbering in the thousands, mountain zebras live in small groups. They seem to be the zebras most closely related to horses. They neigh like horses, unlike the plains zebras who make an unusual, barking sound.

The Grevy's Zebra

The Grevy's zebra is the largest of the three species of zebras. It can stand as tall as 63 inches (160 cm) tall at the withers and weigh as much as 992 pounds (450 kg). It is also easy to tell apart from the other zebras because of its big ears and its delicate black-and-white striping.

form loosely organized groups of different sizes that are constantly changing. In the course of a single day, individual animals can move several times from group to group or remain alone for hours at a time. About 10 percent of adult male Grevy's zebras live in a territory of several square miles. They are visited by mares when it is time to mate.

The Grevy's zebra lives in the bush country and the semi-arid areas of northeastern Africa. It was first discovered and described there by Western researchers in 1882. They decided that the "tiger zebra" that had been mentioned 2,400 years ago by the Greek philosopher Aristotle was in all likelihood a Grevy's zebra. The numbers of Grevy's zebras have dropped sharply in the last few decades. It is now estimated that there are only about seven thousand of these animals left.

The social behavior of these zebras is quite different from that of the other zebras. They

Because of their diminishing numbers, the Grevy's zebras are endangered animals. But with human efforts to encourage these beautiful animals to reproduce under special preserve or zoo conditions, the Grevy's zebras may once again have a growing population.

Top, left: In northern Kenya, one can sometimes see the delicately striped Grevy's zebra (front) together with the plains zebra (rear).
Top, right: Unfortunately, the South African mountain zebra is nearly extinct.

Asses

Height: 36-60 inches (90-150 cm)
Height in hands: 9-15

Perhaps because of its long ears and large head, the ass is a much-maligned member of the horse family Equidae. But to the surprise of many people, this animal is actually more intelligent than the horse. This is especially true of the domestic ass. Its relatives living in the wild include the following:

The Asiatic Wild Ass

It is very hard to decide whether the call of the Asiatic wild ass sounds more like the two-syllable "hee-haw" of a donkey or the warbling neigh of a horse. The animal has the large head of a donkey, but its ears look much more like those of a horse.

In historic Assyrian paintings over three thousand years old, there are representations of hunting and pulling animals that look very much like the Asiatic wild ass. This has led many to believe that the Assyrians tamed and domesticated the wild asses. But it is more likely that these animals were mules. The Asiatic wild ass is not a domestic animal. It is extremely wild, with a mind of its own. This animal can be kept and bred in zoos. However, even the zoo animals that are handled by people on a daily basis never completely lose their distrust of humans, and they never allow themselves to be used for work.

About 51 inches (130 cm) tall and weighing 640 pounds (290 kg), the Asiatic wild ass once had an enormous range. It inhabited the plains, deserts, and arid mountains across all of southern and central Asia. Today, however, it can only be found in a few places. One important reason for this is that the

Asiatic wild ass can live off dry plant growth in the desert, but it must have water to drink at least once every two or three days. In the plains areas of Asia, watering holes are rare. Most water has been claimed for people and their domestic animals. Thus, the Asiatic wild ass has little chance of surviving.

There are seven subspecies of Asiatic wild

The onager, a subspecies of the Asiatic wild ass, can only be found in the wild in Iran.

ass, although two of these — the Anatolic and Syrian wild asses — are already extinct. The other five groups are threatened with extinction. Large numbers of only one type of Asiatic wild ass still exist — the Kiang. It makes its home in the high mountains of Tibet at altitudes of between 4,000 and 5,000 feet (1,220 and 1,525 m) above sea level. The Tibetan people consider these animals sacred and thus never hunt them. In addition, the animals are legally protected by the Chinese government. Nonetheless, the number of Kiangs has been going down, since domestic animals also graze in these high areas, competing with the wild asses for food.

The African Wild Ass

The African wild ass, 53 inches (135 cm) tall at the withers and weighing about 600 pounds (275 kg), is among those animals most threatened with extinction. At one time, they

The beautiful Somalian wild ass is the last surviving subspecies of the African wild ass.

could be found all across the north of Africa, from the Atlantic Ocean east to the Indian Ocean. Today, there are only a few hundred animals left. These are the Somalian wild asses that live in Somalia and Ethiopia. The other two subspecies of the African wild ass, the Nubian and the Atlas wild asses, are believed to be extinct.

The few Somalian wild asses that survive have retreated back into the dry, almost uninhabitable rocky deserts. Although they have nothing there to eat but mimosa bushes, thornbushes, and tough grasses, the animals don't seem to suffer. They are tough animals that actually seem to like this sort of food.

The Domestic Ass, or Donkey

People have seen asses living in the wild in Death Valley in California, on hills of volcanic soil in the Galapagos Islands, and in the dry Australian outback. But as is the case with mustangs, these are not real "wild" asses, but rather domestic animals that have returned to life in the wild.

All the domestic asses in the world are descendants of the African wild ass. Unlike its Asiatic cousin, the African wild ass has a very even temper and can be easily tamed. Apparently, it was already being tamed six thousand years ago in Libya, even before the horse. During the same period or perhaps a little later, the Egyptians also discovered this practical domestic animal. Soon, domestic asses were being used by civilized people everywhere. At least 3,500 years ago, there were already domestic asses in Asia Minor. From there, they traveled to Italy and Greece. The Romans valued them not only as work animals, but apparently also as sacrifices to the gods. The ass was finally introduced into Central Europe sometime during the Middle Ages. Domestic asses eventually came to the Americas with the Spanish and Portuguese conquerors and explorers, where they worked as pack animals in the high Andes Mountains of South America.

Among the main features of the ass is its remarkable toughness. This hardy animal can eat thistles if need be. It is also untiring. It is slower than the horse and thus less prized as a riding animal, but it works hard carrying heavy burdens. The milk produced by the mare is extremely healthy, and in many places it is used as a type of medicine.

Although the ass was domesticated before the horse and can be found almost everywhere in the world, only a few new types have been bred. One of these is the Balkan Ass from

Greece and Yugoslavia, an animal barely 36 inches (91 cm) high. Just as small, but also strong and extremely sure-footed, is the Savoyen Ass that is bred in Alpine areas. The asses that live on the Italian island of Pantelleria are big, slim, spirited, and good for riding. They are the only means of transportation on the island and are often used as breeding animals because of their positive features. The Spanish Giant Ass can be up to 55 inches (140 cm) high, but the largest of all the asses is the Poitou Ass from France. It is over 59 inches (150 cm) high and is especially in demand for breeding mules.

All species of domestic wild asses descend from the African wild ass.

Mules

Height: 48-72 inches (122-183 cm)
Height in hands: 12-18
Weight: 600-1,600 pounds (270-726 kg)

Mules are the result of crossbreeding between female horses and male asses. Animals called *hinnies*, on the other hand, are the product of male horses and female asses. Almost all mules and hinnies are barren, meaning they cannot produce offspring of their own. Only rarely is it possible to breed such a mare.

The mule is reliable, untiring, undemanding — and only sometimes stubborn!

In 1976, the biggest horse race of all time was run during the U.S. bicentennial. The course went from New York to California, covering over 3,728 miles (6,000 km) across North America. Surprisingly, the winners of the race were two mules. They had outlasted two hundred different horses. Mules are extremely strong, and they are pleasant to ride. Historians say that even Napoleon often rode mules instead of his costly Arabians.

Mules have the shape and overall size of a horse and the large head and long ears of an ass. They are sure-footed, more stable, and less moody than horses, which makes them highly valued in mountainous regions. Mules are mainly bred in Spain, France, Italy, and North Africa. Most experts agree that even if they do not have the nobility of thoroughbred horses, the mules have been prized for generations for their strength and friendliness.

APPENDIX
TO
ANIMAL FAMILIES

HORSES

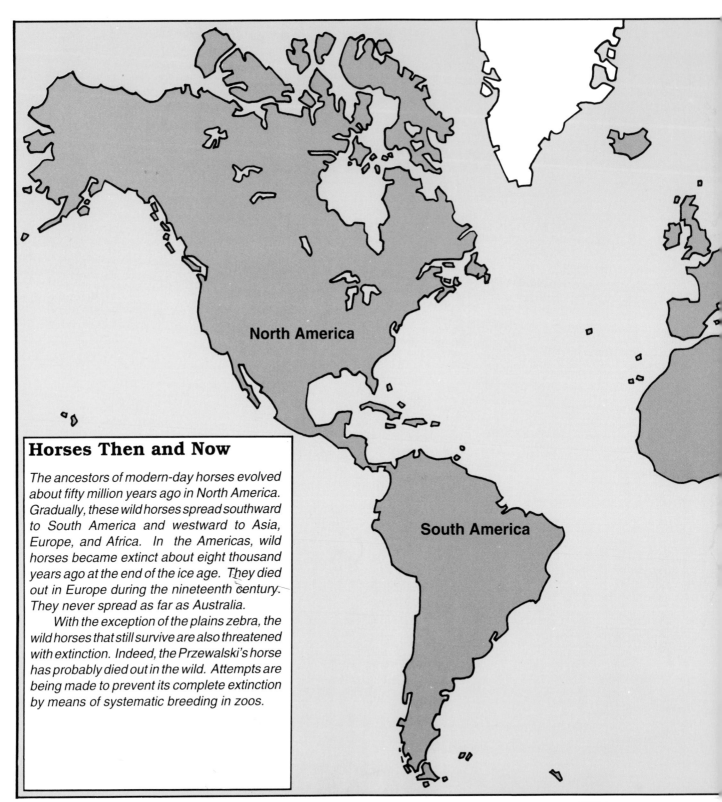

Horses Then and Now

The ancestors of modern-day horses evolved about fifty million years ago in North America. Gradually, these wild horses spread southward to South America and westward to Asia, Europe, and Africa. In the Americas, wild horses became extinct about eight thousand years ago at the end of the ice age. They died out in Europe during the nineteenth century. They never spread as far as Australia.

With the exception of the plains zebra, the wild horses that still survive are also threatened with extinction. Indeed, the Przewalski's horse has probably died out in the wild. Attempts are being made to prevent its complete extinction by means of systematic breeding in zoos.

North America

South America

Przewalski's Horse   Asiatic Wild Ass   African Wild As

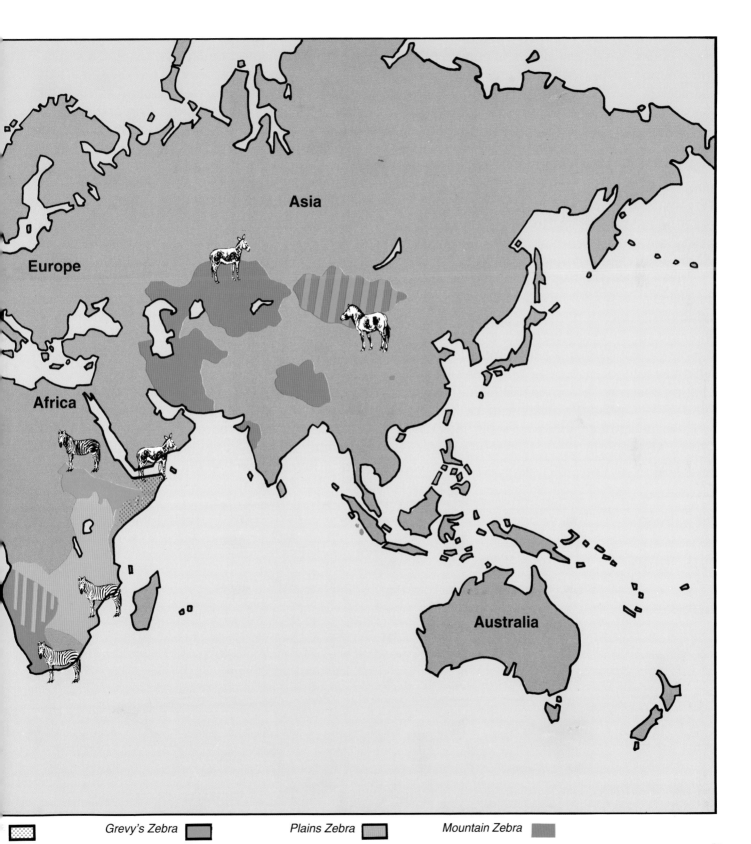

Europe

Asia

Africa

Australia

Grevy's Zebra   Plains Zebra   Mountain Zebra

ABOUT THESE BOOKS

Although this series is called "Animal Families," these books aren't just about fathers, mothers, and young. They also discuss the scientific definition of *family*, which is a division of biological classification and includes many animals.

Biological classification is a method that scientists use to identify and organize living things. Using this system, scientists place animals and plants into larger groups that share similar characteristics. Characteristics are physical features, natural habits, ancestral backgrounds, or any other qualities that make one organism either like or different from another.

The method used today for biological classification was introduced in 1753 by a Swedish botanist-naturalist named Carolus Linnaeus. Although many scientists tried to find ways to classify the world's plants and animals, Linnaeus's system seemed to be the only useful choice. Charles Darwin, a famous British naturalist, referred to Linnaeus's system in his theory of evolution, which was published in his book *On the Origin of Species* in 1859. Linnaeus's system of classification, shown below, includes seven major categories, or groups. These are: kingdom, phylum, class, order, family, genus, and species.

An easy way to remember the divisions and their order is to memorize this sentence: "Ken Put Cake On Frank's Good Shirt." The first letter of each word in this sentence gives you the first letter of a division. (The *K* in *Ken*, for example, stands for *kingdom*.) The order of the words in this sentence suggests the order of the divisions from largest to smallest. The kingdom is the largest of these divisions; the species is the smallest. The larger the division, the more types of animals or plants it contains. For example, the animal kingdom, called Animalia, contains everything from worms to whales. Smaller divisions, such as the family, have fewer members that share more characteristics. For example, members of the bear family, Ursidae, include the polar bear, the brown bear, and many others.

In the following chart, the lion species is followed through all seven categories. As the categories expand to include more and more members, remember that only a few examples are pictured here. Each division has many more members.

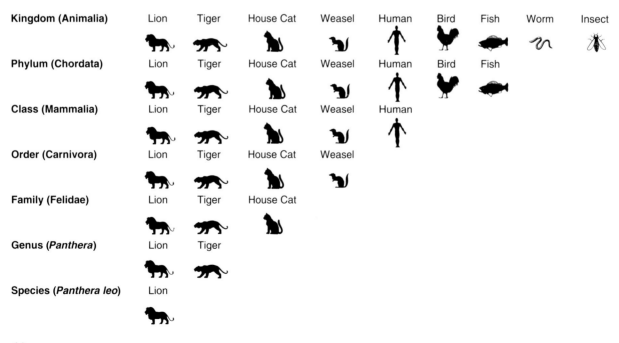

	Lion	Tiger	House Cat	Weasel	Human	Bird	Fish	Worm	Insect
Kingdom (Animalia)	Lion	Tiger	House Cat	Weasel	Human	Bird	Fish	Worm	Insect
Phylum (Chordata)	Lion	Tiger	House Cat	Weasel	Human	Bird	Fish		
Class (Mammalia)	Lion	Tiger	House Cat	Weasel	Human				
Order (Carnivora)	Lion	Tiger	House Cat	Weasel					
Family (Felidae)	Lion	Tiger	House Cat						
Genus (*Panthera*)	Lion	Tiger							
Species (*Panthera leo*)	Lion								

SCIENTIFIC NAMES OF THE ANIMALS IN THIS BOOK

Animals have different names in every language. For this reason, researchers the world over use the same scientific names, which usually stem from ancient Greek or Latin. Most animals are classified by two names. One is the genus name; the other is the name of the species to which they belong. Additional names indicate further subgroupings. Here is a list of the animals included in *Horses*.

Przewalski's wild horse	*Equus caballus przewalskii*	Mountain zebra	*Equus zebra*
Tibetan wild ass (kiang)	*Equus kiang*	Grevy's zebra	*Equus grevyi*
Asiatic wild ass	*Equus hemionus*	Domestic horse	*Equus caballus*
Burchell's plains zebra	*Equus burchelli*	Domestic ass, African wild ass	*Equus asinus*

GLOSSARY

adaptation
When an animal or plant changes in order to better fit into and survive in its environment.

ancestor
Organism from which a plant or animal is descended; a forerunner.

breed
Animals within a species characterized by specific traits and usually limited to individuals that are formally certified as meeting the strict registry rules of a national or international organization.

breeding
To produce a specific type of offspring by mating a certain kind of male with a certain type of female.

class
The third of seven divisions in the biological classification system proposed by Swedish botanist-naturalist Carolus Linnaeus. The class is the main subdivision of the phylum. Horses belong to the class Mammalia. Animals in this class have skin covered with hair, they give birth to live young, and they nourish their young with milk from mammary glands.

cold-blooded
When referring to horses, cold-blooded horses and warm-blooded horses have the same body temperature. In horses, the term *cold-blooded* refers to the horse's temperament. A cold-blooded horse is peaceful, calm, and cool.

colt
A male horse under the age of four years.

crossbreed
To mate a male of one breed with a female of another.

descendant
Offspring that has come directly through a certain line of ancestry, or lineage.

domestic animal
Any of various animals tamed by people so that the animals live and breed in conditions set up by people. Domestic animals are trained to live with and be useful to humans.

equestrian
Relating to or featuring horseback riding.

equine
Of or relating to horses or the horse family.

extinction
The condition of being completely destroyed or killed off. Many animals, like the dodo and the great auk, are now extinct.

family
The fifth of seven divisions in the biological classification system proposed by Swedish botanist-naturalist Carolus Linnaeus. A family is the main subdivision of the order and contains one or more genera. Horses belong to the family Equidae.

foal
A newborn male or female horse.

genus (plural: **genera**)
The sixth division in the biological classification system proposed by Swedish botanist-naturalist Carolus Linnaeus. A genus is the main subdivision of a family and includes one or more species. Horses belong to the genus *Equus*.

herd
A number of animals of one kind that stay together and travel together in a group.

hinny
The result of breeding a stallion with a donkey.

interbreed
To mate with another breed or species.

kingdom
The first of seven divisions in the biological classification system proposed by Swedish botanist-naturalist Carolus Linnaeus. Animals, including humans, belong to the kingdom Animalia. It is one of five kingdoms.

mammal
A warm-blooded animal that nurses its young with its own milk. Whales, humans, and horses are some examples of mammals.

mane
The long, heavy hair around the neck of a horse.

mare
A female horse that is fully mature (over the age of four) or of breeding age.

mate (verb)
To join together (animals) to produce offspring.

mustang
The small, wild horse of the western North American plains. Mustangs are also referred to as *cayuses*, or sometimes *broncos*.

neigh
The loud, long cry that a horse makes.

order
The fourth of seven divisions in the biological classification system proposed by the Swedish botanist-naturalist Carolus Linnaeus. The order is the main subdivision of the class and contains many different families. Horses belong to the order Perissodactyla.

phylum (plural: **phyla**)
The second of seven divisions in the biological classification system proposed by the Swedish botanist-naturalist Carolus Linnaeus. A phylum is one of the main divisions of a kingdom. Horses belong to the phylum Chordata, the group consisting mainly of animals with backbones (vertebrates).

purebred
Bred from horses that are of the same breed.

species
The last of seven divisions in the biological classification system proposed by Swedish botanist-naturalist Carolus Linnaeus. The species is the main subdivision of the genus. It may include further subgroups of its own, called *subspecies*. At the level of species, members share many features and are capable of breeding with one another.

stallion
A mature male horse that is kept for breeding.

subspecies
A subgroup whose members have common features. The specific subspecies is part of a larger species.

warm-blooded
When referring to horses, warm-blooded and cold-blooded horses have the same body temperature. In horses, warm-blooded refers to a horse's temperament. A warm-blooded horse is usually more high spirited and quicker to react than a cold-blooded horse.

whinny
The sound a horse makes in a lower and gentler way than the longer and louder neigh.

withers
The ridge between the shoulder bones of a horse.

MORE BOOKS ABOUT HORSES

Album of Horses. Marguerite Henry (Macmillan)
All About Horses. Marguerite Henry (Random)
America's Horses and Ponies. Irene Brady (Houghton Mifflin)
Draft Horses. Jerolyn Nentl (Crestwood)
Horses and Foals. G. Fern Brown (Franklin Watts)
Horses and Riding. George Henschel (Franklin Watts)
Wild and Wonderful Horses. Christopher Brown, ed. (Antioch)
The Wild Horses. Carl R. Green and William R. Sanford (Crestwood)
Yesterday's Horses. Jean S. Doty (Macmillan)

PLACES TO WRITE

The following are some of the many organizations that exist to educate people about animals, promote the protection of animals, and encourage the conservation of their environments. Write to these organizations for more information about horses, other animals, or animal concerns of interest to you. When you write, include your name, address, and age, and tell them clearly what you want to know. Don't forget to enclose a stamped, self-addressed envelope for a reply.

The American Horse Council
1700 K. Street, N.W.
Washington, DC 20006

American Horse Shows
   Association
220 East 42nd Street
New York, NY 10017-5806

North American Trail Ride
   Conference
1505 East San Martin Avenue
San Martin, CA 95046

People for the Ethical Treatment
   of Animals (PETA)
P.O. Box 42516
Washington, DC 20015

Pennsylvania Horsebreeder's
   Association
203 North Union Street
Kennett Square, PA 19348

U.S. Pony Clubs
893 South Matlock Street, Suite 110
West Chester, PA 19382

THINGS TO DO

These projects are designed to help you have fun with what you've learned about horses. You can do them alone, in small groups, or as a class project.

1. Look in the yellow pages to find the address of a riding stable in your area. Ask your parents to accompany you on a visit there. This will give you a first-hand look at the magnificent horse.

2. Go to the library and check out a book about the pony express. You will be fascinated at how mail was delivered in days gone by.

3. Ask a parent to help you rent a videotape movie that features a horse. Four good choices are *Black Beauty*, *National Velvet*, *The Black Stallion*, and *Phar Lap*.

4. Arrange a visit to a veterinarian who treats horses. He or she can tell you about the medical care of a horse.

INDEX